C000204372

Deptford | Depe Ford

Images from the 1400s to the Present Day

... long and proud history of educating local children ...

Addey & Stanhope School 1715-2015
300 years of service to Deptford.

DEPTFORD CREEK.

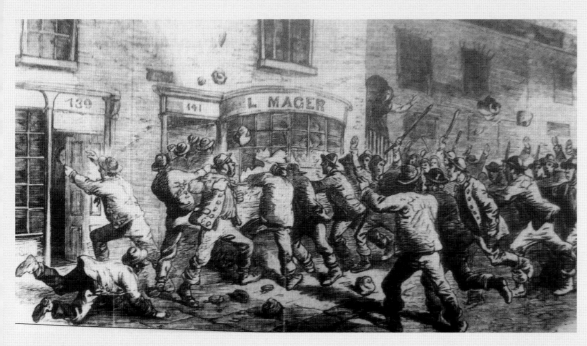

▲ Hunger and poverty led to these scenes on Deptford High Street, known as the Bread Riots.

In 1869 The Contagious Diseases (Animals) Act ▶ became law to provide for the sale and slaughter of foreign animals. Deptford was the first port where this happened on an industrial scale. The women butchering the animals were known as The Gut Girls.

▲ Deptford Central Hall Soup Kitchen. "Growing old with but few experiences of the joys and pleasures of girlhood."

▲ How do we tackle fuel poverty? These awesome local residents organised a meeting at the We Care Food Bank, set up a working party, and signed up churches, schools and community centres who were prepared to allow them to install solar panels on their roof spaces in return for low-cost energy bills. Surplus profit will be used to combat fuel poverty in the community. The South London Energy Co-op is a wonderful example of what we can achieve as a community.

Thanks to the campaign by ▶ local historian Mari Taylor, this park was named after the great man. It is all that remains in the area to commemorate him and his achievements.

◀ Inside Deptford's pioneering power station, known as Ferranti's Light.

Welcome to
Ferranti Park
London Borough of Lewisham

General infor...

Photograph by Jim Rice 1992

▲ Mari Taylor and Helen Garrard rescuing valuable social and technical archives from skips on what was once the site of Deptford Coal Powered Stations, where Millenium Quay now stands.

Sebastian de Ferranti's Light pioneered high-voltage alternating current, which led to the evolution of the National Grid and the modern distribution of electricity.

▲ Deptford Power Station, once the largest power station in the world.

◀ View of where the power station and dock once stood (2014).

▲ The Luftwaffe flying over Deptford in 1943. Deptford docks were heavily bombed, as the river made it easy to navigate and locate targets.

▲ Outside Deptford Town Hall: a long queue of Deptford's young men waiting to sign up for the First World War.

▼ Drawing of Deptford Town Hall today by Dan Strange, local artist and community activist.

▲ Deptford back in the day.

▲ Friendly Park (1950s).

▲ Brookmill Park today.

▲ The last time the old May-Day dance, Jack-on-the-Green, was performed by local chimney sweeps (1907). It will be performed again in May 2015 as part of the Deptford Heritage Festival.

▲ Officials of the Deptford Borough Council distribute blankets and other necessities to victims of the disastrous flood that occurred on 7 January 1926.

▲ Children having fun at the opening of Friendly Park. Unfortunately, the lido has not survived.

▲ South side of Old Flagon Row, looking towards the High Street.

▲ Deptford High Street.

▲ Wooden houses (1888). The sign for The Golden Fleece pub on Mill Lane (now Brookmill Road) is just visible.

▲ Houses on Princes Street.

▲ Watergate Street.

▲ Grove Street.

▲ Broomfield House, Evelyn Street (1839).

▲ Deptford Bakery, Mill Lane (now Brookmill Road) (1841).

◄ Deptford Pier (1841).

◄ St Paul's Church, Deptford High Street.

▲ A rare newspaper clipping of the 15-year-old Ray Barron-Woolford roller skating for War on Want to raise money for the starving in Africa. Ray had no idea that, 40 years later, he would be running a food bank to feed local people in food crisis just two miles from the City of London.

▲ Barbara Raymond and Raymond Barron-Woolford, founders of the We Care Food Bank, with Nicola, the first manager, and Lien, the first volunteer (and Digby the dog). At the start the food bank opened just 2 hours, once a week. Today it is open 6 days a week and is the UK's largest independent food bank. It is entirely supported by donations from the community and receives no government or council funding.

▲ Ray Barron-Woolford.

Photo © 2014 Guy Corbishley (used with permission)

◄ Marie, Nancy, Jess, some of the Saturday team at We Care Food Bank in New Cross, together with Agnes, the founder of the Suffolk branch.

Photo © 2014 Guy Corbishley (used with permission)

▲ With the consequences of the financial crisis bearing down hardest on those who bore little or no responsibility for it, People Before Profit organises The Carnival Against the Cuts to defend local services and jobs, and to demand that proposed developments, such as at Convoys Wharf, address the needs of the local community, not the greed of investors. The Pepys Community Forum has also fought hard over the past 12 years to secure the best deal for the people of Deptford.

▲ John Hamilton with members of Lewisham People Before Profit at Bromley Court. When the Council planned to sell off period homes at knock-down prices at auction, People Before Profit occupied the homes and, after a media outcry, the council backed down and agreed not only to stop the selling off of council houses, but also to build 500 new homes. People Before Profit had demonstrated that direct action can lead to positive results. In 2014 People Before Profit built an eco-house in a matter of days on land that was once the home of hundreds of council tenants but which had been left to the weeds for 10 years after the flats had been demolished. The eco-house project was intended to demonstrate that decent housing can be built both quickly and cheaply, and to raise awareness of the council's failure to address our housing crisis. The night before the new residents were to move in, the council bulldozed the home. John Hamilton was arrested and faced a prison sentence merely for publicising what People Before Profit had done on a fence. In court, John argued that it was not in the public interest to send him to jail and all charges were dropped.

▲ The Bonfire of the Bonds (5 November 2013).

▲ When Lewisham Council planned to close 5 libraries and to sell off our local library to Poundland, Lewisham People Before Profit occupied the library to stop the sale. This picture shows James, a local community activist, Ewa, a Green Party activist, and Louise, chair of Save Lewisham Hospital, in the library. Thanks to their direct action, all 5 libraries were saved.

▲ Paul Phoenix, George Hallam, and Barbara Janiszewska, the three Lewisham People Before Profit Candidates in Evelyn ward, fighting development proposals at the Sir Francis Drake Primary School, Deptford.

Alexia Wdowski, Lewisham People Before Profit's ▲ first political candidate in Deptford, out and about turning what used to be an area where 80% of people voted Labour into a seat LPBP is close to winning.

Launching at Deptford, by John Cleverly (from one of the longest established families in Deptford).

▲ View of Evelyn Street with the Globe public house and, on the left, Prince Street (1841).

▲ E.G. Bernard's House on Deptford Green (1841).

▲ Earliest known image of St Nicholas's Church on Deptford Green, the oldest church in Deptford. Christopher Marlowe is buried here.

◀ Deptford Broadway looking west, by C. Matthews (1840).

Deptford High Street today

The Peasants' Revolt

The Peasants' Revolt, also called Wat Tyler's Rebellion or the Great Rising, was a major uprising across large parts of England in 1381.

The revolt had various causes, including the socio-economic and political tensions generated by the Black Death in the 1340s, the high taxes resulting from the conflict with France during the Hundred Years War, and instability within the local leadership of London. The final trigger for the revolt was the intervention of a royal official, John Bampton, in Essex on 30 May 1381. His attempts to collect unpaid poll taxes in the town of Brentwood ended in a violent confrontation, which rapidly spread across the south-east of the country. People from a wide spectrum of rural society, including many local artisans and village officials, rose up in protest, burning court records and opening the local gaols. The rebels sought a reduction in taxation, an end to the system of unfree labour known as serfdom, and the removal of the King's senior officials and law courts.

Inspired by the sermons of the radical cleric John Ball and led by Wat Tyler, a contingent of Kentish rebels advanced on London. They were met at Blackheath, just yards from the site of the future Battle of Deptford Bridge, by representatives of the royal government, who unsuccessfully attempted to persuade them to return home. King Richard II, then aged only 14, retreated to the safety of the Tower of London, but most of the royal forces were abroad or in northern England. On 13 June, the rebels entered London and, joined by many local townsfolk, attacked the gaols, destroyed the Savoy Palace and the Temple Inns of Court, set fire to law books and killed anyone associated with the royal government. The following day, Richard met the rebels at Mile End and acceded to most of their demands, including the abolition of serfdom. Meanwhile, rebels entered the Tower of London, killing the Lord Chancellor and the Lord High Treasurer, whom they found inside.

On 15 June, Richard left the city to meet with Tyler and the rebels at Smithfield. Violence broke out, and Richard's party killed Tyler. Richard defused the tense situation long enough for London's mayor, William Walworth, to gather a militia from the city and disperse the rebel forces. Richard immediately began to re-establish order in London and rescinded his previous grants to the rebels. The revolt had also spread into East Anglia, where the University of Cambridge was attacked and many royal officials were killed. Unrest continued until the intervention of Henry le Despenser, who defeated a rebel army at the Battle of North Walsham on 25 or 26 June. Troubles extended north to the cities of York, Beverley and Scarborough, and west as far as Bridgwater in Somerset. Richard mobilised around 4,000 soldiers to help restore order. Most of the rebel leaders were tracked down and executed; by November, at least 1,500 rebels had been killed.

The Peasants' Revolt has been widely studied by academics. Late 19th-century historians used a range of sources from contemporary chroniclers to assemble an account of the uprising, and these were supplemented in the 20th century by research using court records and local archives.

Interpretations of the revolt have shifted over the years. Once seen as a defining moment in English history, modern academics are less certain of its impact on subsequent social and economic history. The revolt heavily influenced the course of the Hundred Years War, by deterring later Parliaments from raising additional taxes to pay for military campaigns in France. The revolt has been widely used in socialist literature, including by the author William Morris, and remains a potent political symbol for the political left, informing the arguments surrounding the introduction of the Community Charge in the United Kingdom during the late 1980s and early 1990s.

Richard II meets the rebels on 13 June 1381.
(Miniature from a 1470s copy of Jean Froissart's *Chronicles*.)

COLLECTOR
WINDMILLS

DEPTFORD WINDMILL
and Chapel - Tanners Hill (Drawing dated 1840)

Pamlin Prints
Croydon CR0 1HW

C6115

▲ Back in the day, rich or poor, it was not proper to leave the house without a hat.

SAINT PAUL'S
TO THE
RATE-PAYERS
OF
ST. PAUL'S, DEPTFORD.

Ladies & Gentlemen,

Through the decease of the late Mr. BIGSBY, the situation of

Grave Digger

having become vacant, I beg most respectfully to offer myself a Candidate for the same. My reasons for doing so are (viz.) that having from my Childhood been brought up to the business of a Sugar-mould Potter, but which has now become superceded by the recent invention of Wrought-iron Moulds, I AM

Totally without Employment,

not understanding any other business, by which to assist in obtaining a livlihood for my Family, which consists of

A WIFE AND 8 CHILDREN

nearly all depending upon my WIFE for Support !

☞ My Family and Self have been Rate-Payers for Upwards of 70 YEARS in this Parish ; and I trust that my private character will bear the closest inspection ; I therefore humbly beg your kind Support and Assistance in my behalf, and should I be the fortunate candidate, I will do my utmost for the satisfaction of the parish generally.

I am, Ladies & Gentlemen,
Your humble Servant,

Tanner's-hill, Deptford.
Nov. 13, 1840.

W. COCKLE,

PYRKE, PRINTER, DEPTFORD.

Kath Duncan

Kath Duncan was a legendary communist activist in Deptford in the 1930s. A teacher, she became a redoubtable organiser of the unemployed. She was a powerful orator and a woman with obvious personal magnetism and an attractive demeanour. The local Deptford press felt unable to refer to her without mentioning her "blazing red hair"!

Katherine Duncan was born around 1889 in Scotland, a descendent, she claimed, of Rob Roy, who "would never steal from the poor". In her youth she was much influenced by the suffragette movement and joined the Independent Labour Party in her village.

A teacher and member of the NUT, in 1923 she moved to Hackney in London with her husband, Sandy, who was also a teacher. There they joined both the local Independent Labour Party and the Hackney Labour Dramatic Group. Husband and wife remained ILP members until the 1926 general strike, when they joined the Communist Party.

In 1929 Kath was elected to the party's Central Committee for one term.

Kath and Sandy moved to Deptford in 1930. Soon afterwards, Kath threw herself into work on behalf of the National Unemployed Workers Movement, becoming a powerful and prolific street orator. A small woman who made powerful speeches, she organised deputations of the unemployed, which were often 5,000 strong, to the Deptford Urban District Council offices. Alf Lucas, the Deptford NUWM organiser, would often speak at these events.

Kath herself headed one such mammoth local deputation, which specifically demanded action to clear the slums and provide work. Children on the march held posters saying:

"Daddy's on the Dole". Such was the size of the deputation that the Council was forced to suspend its standing orders.

In 1931, Kath Duncan stood as a communist in the parliamentary elections for the Greenwich constituency.

During May and June of 1932, hundreds of workers frequently marched to the docks (often through the Blackwell tunnel) to urge dockers not to load "murder ships" with military equipment destined for Japan, which was then in the process of invading mainland China.

On one Sunday in June, 1932, a group of marchers returning from a 3,000-strong meeting in Woolwich, at which Kath and Sandy had spoken, were informed by a police inspector that they must stop singing the 'Red Flag'. When they refused, a large number of police appeared and laid into the crowd with batons. They arrested many of the marchers, including Alf Lucas. Sandy Duncan was hospitalised and the events became known locally as the "Battle of Deptford Broadway".

The news of this unprovoked attack was met with great indignation in Deptford. The next day, as a direct result of the police attack, unemployed men at the Unemployed Training Centre went on strike. An eight-thousand-strong crowd gathered on Deptford Broadway, where Kath demanded the dismissal of the inspector. The police responded with a mounted police charge, batons raining down on the crowd.

On Tuesday, the Daily Worker reported "groups of police patrolling about and the place is like an armed camp". Later, pictures of those arrested were sold to raise money for the "defence fund". Some were released in early October. Two of those jailed, Albert Crane, a 24-year-old hosiery worker, and George Childs, a 24-year-old clerk, were met by "a small band of Deptford Communists" on their release from Brixton prison, and went on to address a meeting of 400 people on Deptford Broadway, where they "said they would not be afraid to go back if there was any chance of it doing any good to the working classes of Deptford".

Six months after the main events, on 19 December 1932, Kath appeared in court, under laws originally used against the leaders of the 14th-century peasant revolt, on a charge of being "a disturber of the Peace of our Lord the King". She refused to be bound over or stay out of politics, and was sentenced to six months in Holloway Prison. (Coincidentally, the 76-year-old Tom Mann was in Brixton Prison at the same time for the very same reason!) While in prison, Kath was forced to make shirts which she herself was "convinced no one would wear".

On her release the people of Deptford flocked to greet her on the Broadway. However, the LCC Education Committee wrote to her a few days after her release to inform her they were going to remove her from the list of approved London County Council teachers. A campaign opposing

the attempted victimisation and spearheaded by the NUT and other unions secured 5,700 signatures in Deptford alone, and as a result the attempt to remove her was defeated.

By 1932, Kath was the acknowledged leader of the unemployed in Deptford, and her open-air meetings had become a feature of political life in South East London. She spoke on platforms with the NUWM leader, Wal Hannington, and at a major NUWM rally in Hyde Park in February 1933. She was involved in securing accommodation in Deptford for unemployed marchers from Kent on their way to Hyde Park in October 1932 and, two years later, for 30 unemployed marchers from Scotland.

Kath and the NUWM South East London organiser, Vic Parker, stood as communist candidates in the 1934 LCC elections. She recalled how a bunch of red carnations arrived at the Communist Party committee rooms at Tanners Hill, sent with best wishes from the boys at Surrey Commercial Docks. Kath appreciated the gesture greatly as dockers had once thrown "ochre", a red dye, over her.

In 1935, Kath, now living at Ommaney Road, New Cross, was once again arrested for refusing to move her meeting from outside the local Unemployment Training Centre at Nynehead Street, New Cross, when asked to do so by Police Inspector William Jones. This provided the first test case for the National Council for Civil Liberties, now known as Liberty, which had been founded in 1934 at a time when workers' protests were subject to severe civil-liberty constraints. As disturbances had occurred at a similar meeting over a year earlier, Jones claimed that he was duty bound to prevent it happening again. But this potentially created a precedent that would allow the police to ban any political meeting in public places at will, simply by expressing a fear of disorder.

Not only was Duncan v. Jones [1936] the first case taken up by the NCCL, it was also a landmark in the law on public order. Despite representation from D. N. Pritt K.C. and Mr Dingle Foot MP, Kath Duncan was fined 40 shillings and costs of five guineas. But her case had gone down in legal history: Kath had been about to make a public address, in a situation similar to one in which, a year before, a disturbance had been incited by her speaking, when she was stopped by the police on the grounds that she would destabilise civil peace by the strength of her words. Even though Kath was arrested while peacefully speaking to a small crowd, she was charged with police obstruction.

This raised the question not of the quality of her conduct but of the reasonableness of the constable's understanding of it. What the constable had to evaluate was the reality of the risk of a breach of the peace.

The Chief Justice's judgment at the end of the trial made it clear that the much-vaunted British democracy, in the absence of a written constitution guaranteeing the right of free speech, is merely a construct of propaganda. His view was that "English law does not recognise any special right of public meeting for political or other purposes. The right of assembly is nothing more than a view taken by the court of the individual liberty of the subject." In other words, it all depends! Even so, for much of the rest of the last century, the practical effect of Duncan v. Jones was to support the notion that free speech was an absolute right, unless the situation was genuinely likely to get out of hand. Kath lost the case but won the war for us, at least for sixty-odd years. Of course, in recent years, as the 'war against terror' has taken priority, public order legislation has got tougher. Kath spoke regularly about the threat of fascism and was involved in the famous Battle of Cable Street in the East End as well as the Battle of

▲ The White Swan Inn in Loving Edward Lane (now Edward Street) (1819). It was the house in which the Police Courts were held prior to the establishment of the Greenwich Police Court in 1840. It was also a staging post for the stage coach to Charing Cross. The Old Red Cow Inn (next door but one) marks the site of the old toll house before it was moved to Evelyn Street in 1834.

DEPTFORD CENTRAL HALL BRASS BAND

▲ Deptford Central Hall Band, performing at Porthleven, Cornwall (August 1907).

Bermondsey. On one occasion, the fascists singled Kath out for special attention but, thanks to a tip-off, local anti-fascists were able to chase them off.

Kath was heavily involved in the Aid to Spain movement, organising door-to-door collections on Sundays throughout Deptford and raising £100 towards an ambulance. She also interviewed men who wished to fight in the International Brigade in Spain. Les Stannard was considered too young to fight in Spain but he and other Deptford YCL-ers were inspired by Kath Duncan's commitment.

Sandy died in Scotland towards the end of the war and, by 1945, Kath was working for the local Labour MP, though she was now crippled by arthritis.

Around 1953, Kath's sister took her home to the Scottish village where she was born and it was here that she died in August 1954. After her death, the London District Committee of the Communist Party produced a pamphlet, "Deptford's tribute to Kath Duncan", in which

the author stated: "Where there was a job to do, Kath was always with us... She would march off at the head, leading the way, full of vitality and purpose. She was always a striking and imposing figure with her neat black costume, spotless white collar, and a black, wide-brimmed straw hat, worn at an angle showing her auburn, short-cropped hair".

▲ Deptford Broadway, back in the day.

▲ The Grand Cinema on Deptford Broadway (1920s).

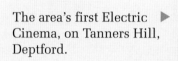

◄ In 2014, local film lovers start a project to open a new independent cinema on Deptford Broadway. This picture shows it at the start of its transformation from a neglected, unloved building to the borough's only cinema.

The area's first Electric Cinema, on Tanners Hill, Deptford. ▶

The Broadway Theatre, on the corner of Deptford High Street and the Broadway (1930s).

▲ The Mickey Mouse Club was extremely popular in the 1930s. This picture shows local residents enjoying a showing at the Grand.

Hussars embarking at Deptford, by the artist William Anderson.

▲ People Before Profit lobby Mayor Johnson at City Hall, insisting that homes be built to address local need not offshore greed. They also demanded jobs for local people, air monitors, and that commercial space be used as a green energy enterprise zone to generate low-cost energy for all local residents, not to house yet more Tesco Metro stores.

▲ John Hamilton, People Before Profit's Lewisham mayoral candidate, launching the Global Day of Action Against Poverty in pouring rain. Deptford pensioners blocked the A20 to highlight the issue, and central London, along with many cities around the world, was brought to a standstill by large crowds wearing masks.

▲ Deptford Green Primary School (2014). Local teachers take part in the national strike to protect pensions and working conditions.

▲ The removal of Deptford's much loved anchor united the entire community in demanding that Lewisham Council give it back. Local artists played a leading role in the campaign.

▲ Anti-PFI campaigners protesting outside Barclays Bank, Deptford. PFI was the main reason the area health trust was declared bankrupt and made it likely that Lewisham would lose its A&E department. People Before Profit launched a huge campaign to make people aware of PFI and explain what it is.

▲ Deptford and New Cross fire stations both faced closure. Deptford's awesome community came together to fight the closure and won. This is the Deptford Fire Crew 2014 taking strike action as part of National strike 2014.

▲ The Save Lewisham Hospital campaign was launched after the government's privatisation plans would have led to the closure of the Lewisham A&E department. 25,000 people marched to stop the closure and twice beat the government in the courts. Community groups such as Lewisham People Before Profit (the only political party in at the start of the campaign), Pensioners' Forum, Keep Our Health Service Public, as well as residents and hospital staff, came together and fought a successful campaign that received global recognition.

▲ Anti-H-bomb demonstration organised by the TUC (15 April 1958). 85-year-old Emma Floyd, the oldest activist in the Deptford Labour Party, leads the marchers to Trafalgar Square, where they were addressed by Bevan and Gaitskell.

Barbara Raymond (widely known simply as 'Mum') is Deptford's longest serving community activist. Tirelessly active in People Before Profit, the Save Lewisham Hospital campaign, DAGE, the Lewisham Pensioners' Forum, the National Pensioners' Parliament, co-founder of the We Care Food Bank and Advice Centre, with over 50 years of never being afraid to occupy, campaign or march to defend the poor, Barbara regularly secures thousands of votes for People Before Profit at election time. When the Labour council wanted to knock down all the Victorian homes in her street, Barbara got organised and, after a 10-year legal battle with the council, her family home was proudly decorated in People-Before-Profit colours and is now the only home on Batavia Road that has not been bulldozed. ▲

▲ Convoys Wharf, until recently known as the Royal Victoria Dockyards. These are views from the latest development proposal (2015).

Battle of Deptford Bridge

The Battle of Deptford Bridge, also known as the Battle of Blackheath, was the culminating event of the Cornish Rebellion and took place on 17 June 1497 on a site in present-day Deptford, South East London, adjacent to the River Ravensbourne. Henry VII had mustered an army of some 25,000 men and the Cornish lacked the supporting cavalry and artillery arms essential to the professional forces of the time. After carefully spreading rumours that he would attack on the following Monday, Henry moved against the Cornish at dawn on his 'lucky day' – Saturday (17 June 1497). The royal forces were divided into three 'battles', two under Lords Oxford, Essex and Suffolk, to wheel round the right flank and rear of the enemy, while the third waited in reserve. When the Cornish were duly surrounded, Lord Daubeney and the third 'battle' were ordered into frontal attack.

Cornish force at the bridge

At the bridge at Deptford Strand, the Cornish had placed a body of archers (using arrows a full yard long, 'so strong and mighty a bow the Cornishmen were said to draw') to block the passage of the river. Here Daubeney had a tense time, before his spearmen eventually captured the crossing with the loss of some men (as few as 8 or as many as 300, depending on one's source). The 'Great Chronicle of London' says that these were the only casualties suffered by the Royal forces that day but, in view of the severity of the later fighting, this seems most improbable.

Due to bad advice or inexperience, the Cornish had neglected to provide support for the men at Deptford Strand bridge, and the main array stood well back into the heath, near to the top of the hill. This was a mistake, since a reserve force charging down from the high ground might have held the bridge bottleneck and made the day a far more equal contest. As it was, Lord Daubeney and his troops poured across in strength and engaged the enemy with great vigour. Daubeney himself was so carried away that he became isolated from his men and was captured.

Astoundingly enough, the Cornish simply released him and he soon returned to the fray. It would appear that, at this late stage, the rebels' hearts were no longer in the battle and they were already contemplating its aftermath and the King's revenge.

Continuation of the battle

The two other royal divisions attacked the Cornish precisely as planned and, as Bacon succinctly put it, "Being ill-armed and ill-led, and without horse or artillery, they were with no great difficulty cut in pieces and put to flight." Estimates of the Cornish dead range from 200 to 2000, and a general slaughter of the broken army was well under way when An Gof gave the order for surrender. He fled but only got as far as Greenwich before being captured. The less enterprising Baron Audley and Thomas Flamank were taken on the field of battle.

Aftermath

By 2pm, Henry VII had returned to the City in triumph, knighting deserving parties on the way, to accept the acclamation of the Mayor and attend a service of thanksgiving at St Paul's.

In due course, severe monetary penalties, extracted by Crown agents, pauperised sections of Cornwall for years to come. Prisoners were sold into slavery and estates were seized and handed to more loyal subjects. The remaining rebels that escaped went home ending the rebellion. An Gof and Flamank were both sentenced to the traitor's death of being hanged, drawn and quartered. However they "enjoyed" the king's mercy and were allowed to hang until dead before being decapitated. They were executed at Tyburn on 27 June 1497. An Gof is recorded to have said before his execution that he should have "a name perpetual and a fame permanent and immortal". Thomas Flamank was quoted as saying,

"Speak the truth and only then can you be free of your chains".

Audley, as a peer of the realm, was beheaded on 28 June at Tower Hill. Their heads were then displayed on pike-staffs ("gibbeted") on London Bridge.

◄ Deptford Bridge today. Its historical importance should be better commemorated.

The Last Pubs
of Deptford

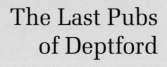

▲ Deptford Broadway looking towards Blackheath (1930s).

▲ Deptford High Street.

▼ Deptford High Street.

▲ Tanners Hill.

▲ Deptford High Street from New Cross Road (1930s).

Deptford Broadway

◀ Deptford Broadway.

▲ Deptford Broadway in 1930.

▲ The Master Shipwright's House, Watergate Street. "The oldest upstanding building – the home and office of the master shipwright since 1513, remodelled in the early 18th century."

Baildon Street. ▶

▲ Deptford Broadway in 2014.

▲ Grove Street (1940s).

Sayes Court work-house (1841). Built around 1725 with materials from the old Sayes Court manor house, by 1852 the building was being used as an emigration depot. In the following year it became a factory for the production of emigrants' clothing, using what was said to be the first sewing machine in England. ▶

▲ The old brewery.

Architect's model of what would ▶
be the Pepys Estate (1960s).

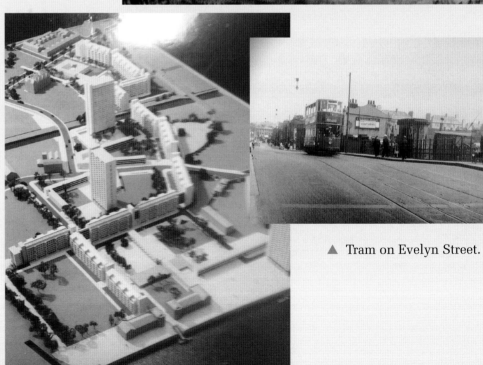

▲ Tram on Evelyn Street.

PETER THE GREAT'S HOUSE AT DEPTFORD (1850).

▲ Workers' cottages on Grove Street, part of Sayes Court Manor. If you walk down Watergate Street you can see the high garden wall and, beyond it, the chimneys of the shipwright's house. This is all that remains of this once grand house and its stunning gardens.

▲ John Evelyn rented his home on Grove Street to Peter the Great, Czar of Russia, who stayed in Deptford for three months to learn about shipbuilding at the dockyard. At the end of his colourful stay, John Evelyn wrote in his diary on 5 June 1698: "I went to Deptford to see how miserable the Czar had left my house after 3 months making it his court. I got Sir Christopher Wren, the King's surveyor, and Mr Loudon, his gardener, to go and estimate the repairs, for which they allowed £150 [a staggering sum of money at the time] in their report to the Lords of the Treasury." 500 Deptford sail-makers, compass-makers, carvers, anchor-smiths, coppersmiths and shipbuilders left with the Czar, first to Holland and then onto Russia, to build the first Russian navy.

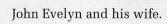

John Evelyn and his wife.

▲ Plan of John Evelyn's gardens at Sayes Court. Today a local group is campaigning to recreate the gardens on a smaller scale, on what remains of the original site, presently a private home.

Radical History Walk

New Cross Gate (start outside Hobgoblin Pub, opposite the tube)

The Red Flag

1889: Jim Connell, an Irishman who had been involved in the Irish Republican Brotherhood and the Land League, writes 'The Red Flag.' Connell worked as a casual docker in Dublin and moved to London in 1875 after being blacklisted for his attempts to unionise the docks. He wrote 'The Red Flag' in 1889 on the train from Charing Cross to New Cross after attending a lecture on socialism at a meeting of the Social Democratic Federation. It was inspired by the London dock strike that was taking place at that time, as well as the activities of the Irish Land League, the Paris Commune, the Russian nihilists and the Chicago anarchists. Connell was a friend of Stepniak, a Russian writer and revolutionary who fled Russia in 1878 after taking part in the assassination of the czarist chief of police.

Woolworth's V2

1944: 168 people are killed on 25 November when a German rocket scores a direct hit on Saturday shoppers at Woolworth's in New Cross (Iceland now stands on the site). Buildings were also destroyed on the other side of the road – hence the prefabs in St James Road. Those killed ranged in age from Michael Glover, aged 1 month, to William Frank, aged 80. The V2s were designed by Werner Von Braun and built by slave labour.

"These rockets are quite similar to some of those they use now. When I see it, I think how vicious, how cool and calculating, how foolish, killing people for some other bugger." (Charles Williams, whose sister and niece were killed in the attack.) Among those who rushed to help at the scene was Dr Harold Moody, a Jamaican GP who lived at 164 Queens Road, Peckham. Moody founded the League of Coloured People at his home in 1931.

28.10.44: 8 killed and 57 injured by a V2 in New Cross (near Pagnell Street).
06.01.45: 10 houses and a church demolished in Kitto Road.
09.01.45: 20 killed in Adolphus Street, Deptford: 'A dazed man walked up and down with a dead infant in his arms, asking where he should put K.'
07.03.45: 52 dead and 64 seriously injured when two blocks of flats were destroyed in Folkestone Gardens on Trundleys Road. (From *Bolts from the Blue: S.E. London and Kent under V2 Rocket Attack* by Lewis Blake (1990).)

Deptford Town Hall

Slavery

Many ships involved in the slave trade and other British imperial activities were built at Deptford. John Hawkins was a pioneer in the development of the slave trade and had a Deptford residence when he became Treasurer of the Navy. In 1567, Francis Drake sailed with Hawkins on a voyage during which 500 West Africans were captured as slaves and transported to the Caribbean after their villages had been burnt and plundered. Drake was later knighted at Deptford by Elizabeth I.

In 1652, Cromwell had been a regular visitor to Deptford to oversee the building of two ships, *The James* and *The Diamond*. These ships formed part of the fleet sent by Cromwell in 1654 to capture Jamaica from the Spanish, where sugar plantations were established and worked by African slaves. After the restoration, Deptford royalist John Evelyn was appointed to the King's Council for Foreign Plantations. Evelyn's mansion was at Sayes Court.

"Arrived at Deptford the 10th of December, where we cast anchor just as it was high water. The ship was up about half an hour, when my master ordered the barge to be manned; and all in an instant, without having before given me the least reason to suspect anything of the matter, he forced me into the barge; saying, I was going to leave him, but he would take care I should not... he swore I should not move out of his sight; and if I did he would cut my throat, at the same time taking his hanger. I began, however, to collect myself and, plucking up courage, I told him I was free, and he could not by law serve me so... just as we had got a little below Gravesend, we came alongside of a ship which was going away the next tide for the West Indies; her name was the Charming Salty, Captain James Doran; and my master went on board and agreed with him for me; and in a little time I was sent for into the cabin. When I came there Captain Doran asked me if I knew him; I answered that I did not; Then, said he, 'you are now my slave'." (From The Interesting Narrative of the Life of Olaudah Equiano: Written by Himself.) 1772: "A Captain at Deptford beat his Negro boy in so cruel a manner that he died."

Goldsmiths College

John Cale

1960-63: John Cale, later of the Velvet Underground, attends Goldsmiths College. He was voted 'Most Hateful Student' by the college's heads of department and caused a minor scandal at an end-of-year concert in 1963 by playing avant-garde pieces of music such as La Monte Young's 'X for Henry Flint', accompanied by Cornelius Cardew and a rowdy audience. *(What's Welsh for Zen? The autobiography of John Cale* by John Cale and Victor Bockris, Bloomsbury, London (1999).)

Malcolm McLaren

1969: Malcolm McLaren attends Goldsmiths College. He advertised a summer festival that entertained thousands of unexpected visitors by claiming that he was 'awaiting confirmation' from Pink Floyd, the Rolling Stones and John Lennon. Dialogued with RD Laing and Alex Trocchi at the festival's final debate. Malcolm was asked to work outside the college for the next two years.
Max Anger: *"On that day the student union hacks - "I'm a moderate!" - were preventing non-student union members from going into the free festival-cum-teach-in. Our little group opened up a side-door and told everybody how to get in. In fact this was far more interesting than what was going on on the stage, which was little more than just a radical version of a chat show... a group of radical women's liberationists disrupted the whole thing, and were treated in a blatantly patronising manner by the stage."* Pistols and King Mob Situationists.
Fred Vermorel, who lived in New Cross: *"I introduced Malcolm to situationism at the 36 bus stop, just outside Goldsmiths College on Lewisham Way."*
1990: Poll Tax - march from Goldsmiths to Lewisham.
1991: 'Shock, Information and the Negation of Control' – a performance by Fred Carter of the Temple of Psychick Youth, involving self-mutilation accompanied by a soundtrack of drones, industrial rhythms and hymns, is cut short.

Clifton Rise

13 August 1977: The National Front assemble in Achilles Street. An all-Lewisham Campaign Against Racism and Fascism marches from Hilly Fields but is stopped by the police. 2000 of the more militant anti-fascists gather in Clifton Rise, where they are baton-charged by police. As the NF enters New Cross Road, there is hand to hand fighting. Clashes with police and NF continue into Lewisham. Police use riot shields in Britain for the first time. 200 people are arrested.

Batavia Road

See the only Victorian house left standing after a 10-year struggle by Barbara Raymond, a lifelong community activist, to stop the Council tearing down her street. It is a testament to her strength and determination that today her house is the only one left on the street. On the other side of Fordham Park, next to the Samaritans office, you can see the former school keeper's house, which Barbara and other People Before Profit activists occupied and successfully prevented the council from selling off this much-needed council home. Now in her 70s, Barbara is still active and a tremendous force for good.

Music

1981: Test Department formed in New Cross in late 1981 by a group of people living at 8 Nettleton Road. They broke new ground as pioneers of a 'metal bashing' industrial sound, using scrap metal for percussion. They played gigs in support of the Miners' Strike, the Printworkers' Dispute (1987), the Ambulance Workers' Strike (1989) and the Anti-Poll Tax Campaign (1990). Their involvement in the Miners' Strike is recorded in the now deleted 1984 LP, *Shoulder to Shoulder*, recorded with the South Wales Striking Miners' Choir, all profits from which went to support the strike. Other local bands from the 70s, 80s and 90s include This Heat, Squeeze, Band of Holy Joy, Blur, and Placebo.

The Moonshot Club, Fordham Park

1975: A sound system is damaged and several arrests are made when police enter and search members of the crowd.
April 1977: The club is occupied by young people after youth workers were accused of having prior knowledge of police raids on young people's homes.
November 1977: A newspaper reports that there had been talk of burning down the Moonshot at a National Front meeting.
18 December 1977: The club is gutted in a firebomb attack and has to be rebuilt.

435 New Cross Road

1926: Headquarters of the General Strike.
8 May 1926: The Deptford Official Strike Bulletin (published by a committee working at 435 New Cross Road) reported, *"Mass pickets posted at most works in the Borough."*
The strike seems to have been solidly supported locally, but as elsewhere middle class strikebreakers were brought in.
This led to police baton charges to clear pickets who were blockading the New Cross Tram Depot (now the bus garage). There were also clashes at a bottle factory on Church Street, as well as on Deptford Broadway, said by the Kentish Mercury (15 May 1926) to be *"rendered almost impassable by a dense crowd."*

439 New Cross Road: New Cross Fire

Sunday 18 January 1981: 13 black youths, all between the ages of 15 and 20, are killed in a fire at a birthday party.
The police reported that the fire was caused by a firebomb, and many believed that it was a racist attack. Racist messages were sent to family members afterwards.

Sunday 25 January 1981: A mass meeting is held at the Pagnell Street Community Centre (formerly the Moonshot Club), attended by over 1000 people. After that meeting, demonstrators marched to 439 New Cross Road and blocked the A2 road for several hours. The New Cross Massacre Action Committee organised a weekly series of mass meetings in New Cross, which came to be known as the Black People's Assembly.

Monday 2 March 1981: The Black People's Day of Action, organised by the New Cross Massacre Action Committee, saw the largest mobilisation of black people ever seen in Britain. 20,000 black people and their supporters marched over a period of eight hours from Fordham Park in New Cross through Peckham, Elephant and Castle, across Blackfriars Bridge, onto Fleet Street, Regent Street, Cavendish Street, and finally into Hyde Park, shouting slogans such as, "Thirteen Dead and Nothing Said;" "No Police Cover-Up!" and "Blood Ah Go Run If Justice No Come." The Sun reported it with the headline, "Day the Blacks Ran Riot in London." Later in 1981: Brixton, Toxteth, etc.

467 New Cross Road

This is the shop, office, meeting rooms, and pop-up book shop of We Care, the largest independent food bank and community advice centre in the country, set up and run by Lewisham People Before Profit activists. The first South London energy co-op to fight fuel poverty was launched here.

Watson Street

The New Cross Empire music hall was situated on the corner of Watson Street.
9 May 1926: Thousands attend a strike meeting at the Empire, featuring the Deptford Labour Choir which leads the singing of the Red Flag. As people leave the meeting, there are clashes with police. That night, a convoy of armoured vehicles passes through New Cross.
1933: Louis Armstrong plays at The New Cross Empire.

New Cross Road

New Cross Road was part of an ancient British trackway, later paved by the Romans and subsequently known as Watling Street (*Wæcelinga Stræt* from the ancient British *Wæcelinga* tribe, through whose territory it passed). Also part of the pilgrims' route to Canterbury. Now the A2.
1930s: British Union of Fascists attempt to reach Deptford and are prevented by a crowd in New Cross Road.
1936: New Cross Road is blocked by 10,000 people marching from Deptford to the Old Kent Road (successfully) protesting against rises in gas prices.
Monday 2 March 1981: New Cross Road is blocked during The Black People's Day of Action.

Deptford High Street

January 1867: at a time of high unemployment, the hungry crowd in Deptford were told that the bread depot, which dispensed bread to the poor, had run out of bread. The crowd headed to Deptford High Street where they sacked a bakers shop; another baker gave away all his bread to prevent a similar outcome. Mounted police dispersed the crowd, but the next day people marched on a meeting of the Poor Law Guardians in Greenwich.

120-122 Deptford High Street (The Job Centre)

The local community fought a long, united campaign to stop the closure of the job centre in an area with 55% youth unemployment. Kept open for 12 months due to direct action, it was finally closed and the building then squatted by the arts collective, Utopia. It has now become a job-centre-themed bar. Lewisham People Before Profit wrote to the owners explaining that the name was offensive and should be changed, while others felt that the name failed to reflect the diversity and vibrancy of Deptford's cultural and artistic communities. The campaign became national news as unions, community groups, the Green Party and others supported Lewisham People Before Profit's position. They will continue to boycott the bar until its name is changed. The owners claim that they always use the previous names of the buildings that house their bars, but the two former local Conservative Party offices they bought are now called Tory Bars, and 120-122 Deptford High Street has been home to the arts collective, Utopia, and The Mercury, a local newspaper. There are certainly other, less offensive names that could be chosen.

Deptford Broadway
1893: Deptford Broadway described as *"a meeting place for idle characters."*
1899: Deptford Broadway described *as "a triangular open space, paved with cobble stones. Stands for barrows and the meeting place of the neighbourhood. Political and other meetings held here."*

Chartists
July 1842: Over 2,000 Chartists gather on Deptford Broadway and even more assemble in Blackheath the following day.
Wednesday 15 March 1848: A mass rally is held by the Greenwich and Deptford Chartists on Blackheath. The Chartist paper, The Northern Star, reports, *"No sooner did the placards announcing the meeting make their appearance, than the minions in power set to work to destroy the meeting, if possible. Hundreds of special constables were sworn in, and the whole of the police from the neighbouring stations were ordered to attend on the day of the meeting, likewise the mounted police from London."*
August 1848: A group of Chartists are arrested for planning an uprising. George Davis, a police informer who had joined the Wat Tyler Brigade of the Greenwich Chartists, gives evidence for the prosecution. As a result, William Cuffay, a black Chartist, is transported to Tasmania.

Gasworkers
George Julian Harney (1817-1897) born in Deptford on 17 February 1817, the son of George Harney, a sailor. Harney was one of 59 Chartists tried at Lancaster in 1843 for taking part in the 'Plug Riots' in Manchester in August and September 1842. He started the *Red Republican* and other papers, met Marx and Engels, and was a member of the Brussels Communist Correspondence Committee. An influential English workers' leader, Harney was known as a left-wing Chartist.
1889: A strike at the South Metropolitan Gas Company on the Old Kent Road and in Deptford.
11 May 1889: A half-mile-long procession of gas workers, accompanied by a brass band, converges on Deptford Broadway calling for an 8-hour day. This was conceded.
December 1889: A no-strike clause is introduced. Union scabs, workhouse inmates and prisoners live in corrugated iron huts inside the works. William Derry, a striking stoker, gets into a fight at the Dover Castle pub after he took two herrings and a haddock from a scab's pocket. George Livesey, chairman of the South Metropolitan Gas Company, creates the Telegraph Hill Park in New Cross as part of an attempted non-union, paternalist deal with the gasworkers.

Women's Suffrage
May 1908: The Lewisham branch of the Women's Social and Political Union, very active in Deptford, speak to a crowd of between 4,000 and 5,000 working men and women on Deptford Broadway, hold a similar size meeting on Blackheath, and another meeting in the New Cross Hall.
1912 and 1914: Women's Social and Political Union take direct action. Post boxes are set alight and blown up in Deptford, Greenwich, Brockley and elsewhere, while fires are set at Dulwich College and in a cricket pavilion in Burnt Ash Road. The press blame the Suffragettes for a fire at St Catherine's Church on Telegraph Hill, but this was never proved.
December 1912: May Billinghurst, a founder of the Greenwich branch of the WSPU in 1910, is jailed for 8 months for an action against a letter box in Blackheath. Billinghurst was a disabled wheelchair user who lived at 7 Oakcroft Road, and was responsible for a number of so-called letter box 'outrages.'

Anarchists
In the 1890s, the Deptford anarchist group is one of the most active in the country, said to have 100 members.

New Cross Bomb Outrage
August 1894: A post office is blown up at 117 New Cross Road, the first of several such attacks in South London. A message, written in French, was found at the site: *"À la mémoire de Racachol, Bourdin, Vaillant, Henry et Sante. Vive l'Anarchie!"* [*"In memory of Racachol, Bourdin, Vaillant, Henry and Sante. Long live Anarchy!"*]
April 1897: Rolla Richards, a member of the Deptford Anarchist Group, is sentenced to 7 years in jail for these attacks.

Kate Sharpley
Kate Sharpley was born in Deptford and had been in the anarchist movement in South London from just before the First World War. She worked for a German baker in South London but worked in a munitions factory in Woolwich during the war and was one of the first shop stewards. Kate's father and brother were both killed in action, while her boyfriend was conscripted and not heard of again. Months later, when Queen Mary was handing out medals in Greenwich, most of them for fallen heroes and being presented to their womenfolk, Kate, then 22, having collected medals for her dead father, brother and boyfriend, promptly threw them back in the Queen's face, saying, "If you think so much of them, you can keep them!" The Queen's face was scratched and so was that of one of her ladies in waiting. The police, not a little under the influence of patriotic propaganda, grabbed Kate, later described by the local press as being under the influence of anarchist propaganda, and beat her up. No charges were brought, but when she was released from the police station a few days later, she was scarcely recognisable.
After her clash with the police, she was sacked from her job on suspicion of dishonesty – nothing had gone missing but a policeman had called "to check up on her." Then, while selling libertarian pamphlets on the street, she was recognised by a policeman and warned that, if she appeared there again, she would be charged with soliciting as a prostitute.

The Unemployed
1931: 5,000 unemployed people march on The Town Hall.
1932: Police order a group of people on Deptford Broadway to stop singing the Red Flag. The order is ignored, the group is baton-charged, and 6 people are arrested. The next day, unemployed workers in local training centres go on strike. 5000 assemble on the Broadway and defeat and scatter the mounted police. Later that year, Kath Duncan of the Deptford NUWM is jailed for a month.
October 1932: Marchers from Kent stop off at Deptford on their way to County Hall. Police stop the march before it reaches its destination and there is fighting around Waterloo as the police forcibly try to break up the crowd.

Deptford Bridge
1381: The peasants revolt against a new poll tax that would mainly hit the labouring classes. 60,000 rebels from Kent set up camp at Blackheath, where they are addressed by the radical preacher John Ball, who argues that all things should be "held in common." The peasants destroy prisons and kill the Archbishop of Canterbury before the rebellion is crushed and thousands of rebels are killed, including their leader, Wat Tyler, who was killed by William Walworth.
1450: Jack Cade leads the Kentish rising against excessive taxation of the common people. As in 1381, they establish a camp at Blackheath. Later they move their headquarters to the White Hart in Borough High Street, Southwark. After a bloody battle on a burning London Bridge, the rising was defeated.
1497: 5,000 Cornish rebels march on London in revolt against a new tax to pay for King Henry VII's planned invasion of Scotland.

They are joined by sympathisers from Devon and Somerset on route. The rebels reach Blackheath Common on 16 June 1497. The following day, English troops surround the area around Blackheath Common and are ready to attack the Cornish soldiers holding Deptford Bridge. The rebellion is crushed on the following day, 17 June 1497. The rebellion is at an end. Two hundred Cornishmen and eight of the King's soldiers are killed. The Cornish leaders An Gof and Flamank "enjoyed" the King's mercy by being hanged until they were dead before being disembowelled and quartered. Their head's were then stuck on pikes on London Bridge.

The Oxford Arms / The Birds Nest
Here flows the river Ravensbourne, otherwise known as Deptford Creek: vital but invisible.

47 Creek Road
The 1970s saw the rise of racism in Deptford and the escalation of the National Front. The Albany tried to counter this with its very popular "Rock Against Racism" gigs, a three-day "All Together Now" festival, a benefit to scrap the sus laws and a successful anti-racist show called "Restless Natives". On 14 July 1978 the Albany was gutted by fire. The next day notes were pushed through the door of the shell on Creek Road saying "GOT YOU". Not all members of the community had appreciated the Albany's efforts to improve race relations.

Deptford Creek
June/July 1998: Resonance FM (London Musicians Collective), temporary radio station. Running throughout Resonance FM was Peter Cusack's London Soundscape. Listeners were asked to send in or tell of their favourite London sounds. It included a recording of Deptford Creek, particularly memorable with the power station hum and the Thames brought together.

Giffin Street
Charles Booth found this area to be one of the poorest in London: Addey Street: "Some prostitutes and criminals, low rough class. The Inspector reckons that this is the worst part of Deptford." Giffin Street: "Many of the houses at the east end are dilapidated and boarded up. Slatternly women standing about, some shoeless children. Low class, some prostitutes, hawkers etc." Irish streets – "the block between the Railway and Hales Street" (including Giffin Street) "Baildon Street – if any men and women have the criminal brand upon their faces, these seem on my two visits unmistakenly to bear it.

Crossfields Estate

Murals
1707: site of a House of Correction (a prison for paupers and vagrants). Became a workhouse in 1926. Another workhouse was built soon after in Sayes Court.
Rules of St Nicholas's Workhouse: *"Rising bell at a quarter before six, at six prayers and afterwards employment, retiring to bed at nine, children at eight. Breakfast shall be at 8, the dinner hour at one, and supper at 7. All other hours shall be considered working hours. No person permitted to leave the house... Grown persons who shall refuse to work shall be confined and kept on bread and water."*
1727: The parish of St Nicholas paid a waterman to *"carry out of town... a big-bellied woman almost ready to lye-in, she carrying two children with her"* to prevent her being a 'burden' on the poor rate.
1848: An inquest is held at the Royal Oak, Deptford High Street, found that Thomas Sturges Nichols, a labourer aged 50, had died of starvation *(Illustrated London News, 15 January 1848).*

McMillan Street

Rachel McMillan Nursery
Margaret and Rachel McMillan were two middle-class socialists who opened the first open-air nursery school in Deptford in 1914. In the 1880s they met William Morris and Peter Kropotkin, and were involved in supporting the 1889 dock strike. They were members of the SDF and the ILP. They also opened school clinics in Evelyn Street and on Deptford Green.
1911: Margaret McMillan publishes *The Child and the State,* in which she criticises the tendency of schools in working-class areas to concentrate on preparing children for unskilled and monotonous jobs. Instead of this, Margaret argues that schools should offer a broad and humane education.
25 March 1917: Rachel McMillan dies.
29 March 1931: Margaret McMillan dies.

Flaggon Row
"In Deptford, near a Place called Flaggon Row, dwells one Anne Arthur, that had a long time got her Living by selling things about the street, who, according to her own report, had diverse Discourses with the Devil on the Third of this Instant March 1684, who offered her Gold and Silver; telling her many strange and Wonderful things; and, in the end, carried her in the Air a Quarter of a Furlong... She has been a notorious Liver, often given to swearing, and calling upon the Devil; breaking the Sabbath, and the like."

▲ Albury Street SE8, formerly Union Street, off Deptford High Street, the only SE8-postcode street where homes now fetch £1.2 million.

Jack-in-the-Green
c. 1903: Police suppress 'Jack-in-the-Green', the chimney sweeps' May Day festival, which featured *"The Deptford Jack, in his tower of greenery... surrounded by traditional dancing and music-making attendants."*

The Horn Fair
17th and 18th centuries: 18 October, people march from Cuckold Point in Bermondsey, through Deptford and Greenwich, and on to Charlton with horns on their heads, the men dressed as women. The fair is banned in mid-19th century after a fight between dockers and army cadets.

St Nicholas's Church
1362: Richard Whyche, priest of St Nicholas's, is burnt at the stake for being a Lollard. He is commemorated by a plaque in the church.

Marlowe

30 May 1593: Christopher Marlowe is stabbed to death in Deptford. He is commemorated by a plaque in the churchyard. Various theories have been put forward as to the circumstances of his death, with suggestions ranging from that he was caught up in the power struggles of the Elizabethan secret state to that he was a heretic and freethinker. After Marlowe's death, Richard Baines, an informer, claimed in a note to the Privy Council that Marlowe had said that *"All they that love not tobacco and boys are fools"* and proclaimed the heresy *"that Saint John the Evangelist was bedfellow to Christ and leaned always in his bosom; that he used him as the sinners of Sodom."*

Deptford was home to many of the first black Londoners. Church burial records:
1692: an Indian called 'Cobit' is buried; 1724: Thomas Berry, a 'Negro Mariner,' is buried; 1726: George Jameson, 'a black man from on board ship'; 1783: Manuel Le Ceasar and Domingo Antonio, two black men, are buried.
1721: A 'free Negro' seaman from Deptford leads *"a Mutiny, that we had too many Officers, and that the work was too hard, and what not."*

The Docks

Pirates
27 February 1696: Captain Kidd sails from Deptford on his ship, the *Adventure Galley*.

Royal Naval Dockyard
1513: Henry VIII establishes the royal dockyard in Deptford.
1739: Workers at Deptford shipyard go on strike when management prevent them from taking home 'chips', bits of wood left over from ship building. Part of the process of increasing the control over the working day, it leads to new laws against 'stealing' from work and the construction of a brick wall around the shipyard.

Sailors' Uprising
1774: Sailors on a warship at Deptford, fed up of going without pay and rations, come ashore to take what food they can from market gardens and farms; five are arrested. 300 armed sailors storm the watchhouse at Deptford Broadway to release some of the prisoners. They are joined by sympathetic local people and a 2000-strong crowd marches on Greenwich to break open the watchhouse where the remaining prisoners were being held. The

▲ The Midi Music Centre, Watson Street, formerly the local morgue. The centre will celebrate its 21st anniversary as part of the Heritage Festival events in May 2015.

sailors were said to have sworn *"most bitter oaths that they would hang in the market place at Greenwich every magistrate and constable they could find."*
1779: A conspiracy to set alight the shipyards is exposed by an informant, a Deptford sailmaker.
1795: Workers go on strike all along the river until a shipwright taken by the press gang is released.

Gut Girls
1879-1913: The Corporation of London's Foreign Cattle Market for the Import and Slaughter of Animals is located at Convoys Wharf, on the site of the Royal Dockyard. Many of the workers were young women known as Gut Girls, whose job was to clean out the innards of the slaughtered animals. Their financial independence, behaviour and taste in clothes were a source of moral panic for 'respectable' locals, and there were complaints that they spent their wages on outlandish hats instead of underwear. A Deptford Fund Committee was set up to train the 13-16 year-old girls in the essential arts of cookery, laundry, needlework, dressmaking and simple matters of hygiene. The intention of all this instruction was to prepare the girls for more suitable and ladylike employment, and perhaps even for marriage. The Albany Institute, which opened in 1899, grew out of this work.

Convoys Wharf
1986: During the News International strike, Convoys supplies newsprint to Rupert Murdoch's company. Striking printers and the Lewisham Print Support Group hold pickets at Convoys Wharf on Friday mornings from 6.30am.
A report of one such picket on 18 April 1986 said: *"About 60 printers and the Lewisham support group picketed Convoys Wharf at King's Street, Deptford. There was some contact with drivers but not much, due to hostility of T&G stewards. Some delay was caused."*
2 June 1986: Major fire at Convoys Wharf.

East India Company
The Stowage site was the base for the East India Company until 1782.
18th century: The East India Company eventually dominates most of India with its own private army and trading monopolies in salt, tobacco, opium and other commodities.
1769-1770: The East India Company creates *"famine over wide areas by cornering rice and refusing to sell it except at exorbitant prices."*

Millennium Quay

Peter the Great
January 1698: Peter the Great, Tsar of Russia, comes to Deptford to study shipbuilding with a view to constructing a modern Russian navy. To finance his military campaigns and domestic reforms, Peter imposes high taxes on the Russian people, including the infamous beard tax. He also deals harshly with people who oppose the reforms and forces many Russians to work against their will in his mines and factories and on his building projects. Peter also extends serfdom, the system under which the majority of Russian peasants lived in conditions little better than slavery. A suitably ugly statue in front of Greenfell Mansions now commemorates his stay.

Gentrification of the river
2005: Tenants on the Pepys Estate protest against the sale of the 29-storey, social-housing block, Aragon Tower, to property developers keen on cashing in on its impressive riverside views.